BOOKS BY KATHERINE HOSKINS

EXCURSIONS

EXCURSIONS

NEW & SELECTED POEMS

KATHERINE HOSKINS

NEW YORK   ATHENEUM   1967

Of the new poems in this book, *Da Ming, December, Honi Soit, Success, The Game, An Environment, Explication de Texte,* and *Now Plus Then* were originally published in POETRY; *The Byfield Rabbit, A Wedding in the Country, In Praise, The Life of Action* and *An Education* first appeared in THE YALE REVIEW.

FOR CAMILLA

EXCURSIONS

Contents

FROM OUT IN THE OPEN

EXCURSIONS

FOR THE INHERITORS

Compassion bends us to our young
Who, in a slant-eyed glance, betray
Their old old selves.
To them we yearn, we cry—
Pushing the hair back from their solemn eyes—
No, no. Be children still.
In spite of us, your world and you are young.
Go, go. Go play.

Play? They answer
As wanting to please us, only our words
Slip by them like the cries of strange birds
Long long ago and in another world
And even there scarce heard.
Play, dear Elders? they repeat their duty.

At ease in summer chairs,
We watch the westing sun pick out
A stark oak limb
From frolic foliage,
Its massive corrugations rosy-lit.
Moved by that sudden bareness note
The strength, part true part fabulous, of oak.

AN ENVIRONMENT

Down in the basement with the bargain-hunting
Parents—while they prowl wild-eyed
Piles of glad rags, piles of mourning weeds,
Ill-fitting, out of date and very dear—
The children scamper mud-coloured fields
Of floor, ancient in grime and cambered like
An oily sea. Half lost amid incessant
Legs and feet, they play they've lost each other—
Hide back of night-gowns dripping off a counter,
Under a fallen coat or skirt; there mute
And breathless stay till found. Interminably,
Found and finders start the game again;
For as the big ones put on parent masks,
Files of babies stagger to the gaps.

Each time there's one at least who's never found.
His game is played for keeps. Lonely, lost,
He reconnoitres from festooned lair,
Stretches a grimy hand, then snatches back
As passionate want that he be found gives way
Before want not. He bites his nails awhile . . .
An upward glance, above the dust-refracted
Glare, stops at a face and eyes intent
On him; mild eyes, calm as statues'. Down head
Vision slides to immobile, carved
Feet, awash in trampled finery.
Chewed hand, respectful, eager reaches them;
Reports flesh, bones and coursing warmth,
A liveable solitude, whole-hearted want.

4

PITY AS POWER

With us, everybody (albeit well known
For a bastard and son of a bitch) is 'a great feller.'
Yet I have never heard a good word said
For Louis Guevin.
It's not just that he was puny in stature,
Mean in feature,
Evil in nature
And by profession idle.
He was dirty. Dirty in body,
Dirty in habit (pee in the kitchen sink
And never a faucet turned on afterward)
And certainly in mind.
He was also a souse (three cans of beer
For breakfast, just as a starter),
A wife-beater and plate-smasher.
Coward, liar and chiseller goes without saying.
The only possible plus in his make-up
Was a tongue like a whip-lash
That he used chiefly on his daughter.
O, Daddy, please—for sixteen years entreating.
Yet never a word against him—
Only as if she were sorry for him.
(From what far peak of sorryness, I've wondered)
And when one judge or another
Would offer to ship him away,
"To give you people some rest",
She'd always beg him off.
No use for us to argue.
A gentle girl, she could be downright mulish.

At any rate, when he died
Everyone, daughter included,
Was greatly relieved.

In our neighborhood, no one thinks
In very grandiose terms.
With us, just one louse less
Is cause for congratulation.
So we were all very cheerful at the idea
Of not having to deal with *him* any more.

However—
It may have been the second
Or the fourth day after his interment,
This Guevin came back.
He returned.
His poor little daughter came on him—
Sitting as usual, she said,
In their apartment.
That would mean slumped in a ratty chair,
Knees spread, malevolent little eyes
Flicking here, flicking there,
His tongue slick with foulness to spit at her.
She wasn't she says, afraid
But apprehensive—a prudent attitude
For anybody facing Guevin.
He didn't speak (and maybe that was the miracle.
Maybe we should hold on right here with that),
But stayed about ten minutes,
She across from him in silent apprehension.
Then he left,
By the front door like anybody else.
She opened it immediately after him
But there was no one in the hall,
No sound on the stairs, and the skylight closed.
I believe she called out Daddy once or twice.

The joke was on us all right—
That this in all ways vile little man,
This et cetera
Should have been permitted to effect,
Or somehow did effect,
(Or was effected for him)
What noble, true and loving men have
(With one notable exception) failed at.

The laughter was sour at best
And soon stopped as we considered
That though the Welfare people had issued
Quantities of tranquilizers to the daughter
(And, so far, they seemed to work)
This might yet be a case for stronger measures.

If so,
We're all agreed it's no job
For the local priest.
It will take a Monsignor
(Myself, I'd prefer a Bishop)
The day we exorcise Louis Guevin.

FOR TAZIO

The royal quality
Of this child's beauty
Gives me who wait on him
Such inordinate pleasure
As, from Rome to Delft,
Those painters must have felt
Who drew so close to nature
The nature of cherubim

PERHAPS TO PROFIT

So now I put away my books
And take up childish things again—
Cry 'Boo', elaborate with blocks.
Now I bend my spirit, branch
It down in birch-leaf-bright detail
To please a child.
                 Does the bent branch
Let go always spring back to its birds?
Shall I who frolic room to room
After the interim find excellence
In hours spent immobile weighing words?
Or, will the babble of babyhood,
My delight in it, deafen me?
Will body's tiredness after the long day
Persist? The emptiness
Of spirit spent on another
Into thriftier times persist?

Like activities induce
Like attitudes. So, at day's dark
Slack on a kitchen chair and idle hands,
I more than recollect,
I half turn into calm-faced amber girls
And crag-cut gardeners. Half into who reared me,
Slack for a moment between chore
And chore (how long to read
What skipping childhood glimpsed)
My guardians inform me with
Repose and grace of patience.
In wide-spaced, old-time cadence murmur,
Take   your   time   child.   Take   your   time.

9

AN EDUCATION

There on the outskirts of the Hansel-Gretel—
Rose-Red—Snow-White wood, there
Where travelers repair to doff their wingèd
Shoes, their magic hats and other fairy
Gear; then put on business suits and with
Corrected sextants sight the sun and moon;
Old Mother Must, Beldame Necessity,
The prime official of this customs hut,
Prepares for guests.
     For the woman she has reared
(Nurse, enemy, now quasi-friend)
She brews a strong and soothing tea, stirs
For the little boy her grand-son sweetened bread,
The sugar nicely measured with his years.
(Though sparse, Must's provender's enlivening).
And greets them heartily. For few so cheerful
Scramble down her hemlock shadowed path
And fewer still say thank-you for her food.

The boy munches bread, the crones drink tea
And tell him tales of his inheritance,
His great demesne. Then say,
     Now go.
Climb the glass mountain, wake the princess,
Learn to scatter stones instead of bread.
Go now, take possession of your land.

He scampers off, glad to be shut of them.
For he is Boots, the Youngest Son, the Prince.
And he has far to go and high to grow
Before he'll think of them again. And yet,
Their farewell, minatory word, Be back

10

By dark, will kindly echo through his troubled
Travels in guaranty of safe return.

Once he's gone, the woman, old and more
Than a little mad from life-long study
Of her darling's realm, expounds his character.
She finds it sturdy.
He'll learn the easy lessons easily—
Not to pick up pine cones where the swart
Dwarf exacts the dearest bread-trough payment;
Always to be kind to beggar women;
If poor and also candid, find
A loyal cat to help him trick the King;
Give Beauty jewels, dresses, furs,
But never pluck for her the living rose.
O, he's bound to learn invaluable
Rules of conduct from those addle-pates—
Useful as Plutarch's . . . She's certain he'll make out.

Out there, says Mother Must, they mostly do.
It's when they get back here the trouble starts.

Then please, dear nurse, dear enemy, half friend,
(When he returns I'll not be here)
When he returns, be kind to him.

Though fluent for her needs, there're many words
That Mother Must has never learned.
She simply has no use for them.
Kind—unkind, the terms embarrass,
Ask for what she's ignorant to give.
I'm not Providence, she mumbles,
Merely a servant, civil more or less.

The woman bites her lips. She knows she's made
A foolish, fruitless plea—but's anxious still.

11

What can Must say that Grand-ma wants to hear?
She searches her pocket for the mirror
That reflects her beautiful, beneficent,
Our Lady Necessity.
And fingering it, she wonders when
She'll be allowed to quit
Her witch disguise, so darned and dowdy,
Steely-faced—and wryly states:
It's somewhat up to him how I'll appear.
Then fetches down the ancient book
And opens it where both can read.
The tales, the same the little boy
Just heard and that he's living now,
From A to Z, are written backward here—
From Z to A—as wisdom flows.
And all who come back from the magic wood
And stoop to Must's low door
Learn to read them so.
Children once again, at old Must's knee
They find out where they went and what they did.

The woman flicks the pages, catching
Ends and starts she well recalls:
How young they are who study here—

The fortunate—

    Nor old on leaving, yet
Not young any more.

    I've never understood,
Says Must, the value put on youth.
(She has her pride of pedagogue).

It's pretty, maybe nothing more.
I hope, she falters, Luck won't leave him
Drift until, a soldier sadly wise,
He's chose the eldest dancing princess.
I hope he won't be one who never
Got to Bremen.

              Must stays mum.
How can she tell till he return
What stories will be true for him.
She fidgets and edges out of doors, across
The grass to where the steep path starts.

The woman dallies: If he climbs
The glass mountain, reading back
He'll find he shared his last resort
With someone poor and old. He'll find,
She pleads, he once outsmarted trolls.
He'll know, for sure, a moment's satisfaction?

If he should climb, says Must, he'll know
A moment's satisfaction.

              The woman sighs
And starts the long ascent. Then, turning,
Points at small birds loud
And active in the hemlocks. Gay
Herself with hope: Perhaps he'll be that Prince
Who understood the speech of birds and was
Advised by them. Perhaps he'll win that way.

If he should win by traffic with the birds
He'll find, on reading back with me,
He ate a human heart the night before.
At best his own.

At best his own!
The woman wails and scrambles up the path.

A WEDDING IN THE COUNTRY

Across the Protestant-white wall,
The pale pattern of leaf-shadows suddenly flurried
And the two children being married,
Along with the black-robed ministeress,
Were left alone to their business.

For every kinsman, child and friend
Especially gathered there to attend
On them had glanced aside through clear North windows
To where these little twisters blow,
To where the prime, the five-point

Stag sleeps under the hill. The beast had stirred,
Clearly; had, though by little, disturbed
The trees; but this time neither leaped
And run . . .

          A subsidence like leaves then
As all faced forward to the old pattern.

THE BYFIELD RABBIT

These white-clay pits of Byfield—
Small, intensively worked—
Scarcely disturbed the grass,
The woods not at all. There,
Shadows changed the kilns
To grossly chimneyed castles,
Suitable for dwarves.

Summer, you'd see the wheels
Outside the huts, lugged
Under the lark-strewn sky
Where light winds plied the meadow.
Then wheel-whir, bee-hum, bird-song
In single sound arose,
And fell, like oars in water.

The clay renowned, the potters
For vases, birds and small
Familial animals.
A Byfield Rabbit was
A term for excellence.
You'd think young princesses,
But grown men collected them.

Stranger, repose yourself
On tufted sun-warmed grass
And think of watery sound
Until it's spread so wide
A rabbit rushes by you.
His own ears quivered back,
Stare-eyed, stretched-out-skinny,
Rab runs a vanished course
Of potters treadling clay;

Clay his great-great-grandsire
Leaped into and there,
Enporcelained, became
A term for excellence.

HONI SOIT

All night we said, This violence
Of sledge-wind, stroke on stroke,
Will blast and up-end our noble, our heritage oak;
Will crash it—immense
Weight, length and leafage—onto the roof-tree.
We'll be ruined, surely.

A wan and drift-cloud morning showed
Hale heritage.
But, on its top-most bough, bleak as an adage,
A carrion crow
Crouched as if always and Honor, Honor cackled.
We did despair then, wholly.

And so we praise those little birds,
Those brave who swooped and pecked
And shoved till mincing, grudging step by step
That rusty sir
Took flight, his Honor rattling; they after, piping
Courage and Love and Charity.

SUCCESS

Try never to get up abruptly and leave.
Unthoughtful action is usually rude,
Often unkind, and can result
In grave disservice to yourself.
Instead, while your companion pokes
At the ground with a stick or spears a leaf,
Contrive a straw man or, if you like,
A carved—some fairly adequate image
Of yourself—and ease it between you.
Then, very gently, make your departure.
Not being liable to close inspection,
It needn't be a speaking likeness.
Any old scarecrow will do, provided
It lend an ear and cast an eye.
Aim for a posture of attentive listening.
If you always take pains to do this,
Beds, benches, stone-walls, kitchens,
Candle and moon light, wherever acquaintance
Or friend has disburdened and rested himself,
Will bear tangible witness to you.
To all intents and purposes, you
Will be, will exist in those places.

Neglect this simple precaution
And you're likely to drift through the world—
In one door and out the other—
Weightless and inconsequential;
A last cricket before winter,
An *ay-mi* wailed by flapping
Streamers of the sheavèd corn.

You must, of course, care for your images—
Trim them up from time to time—
A chore for rainy days.
Yet so, by slow accretion, they
Will merge in men's minds to a single
Bulky figure of many aspects.
Thanks to them, you will be, will have been—
As I said, straw or carved doesn't matter
Unless to yourself—a person of substance.

THE GAME

With years we grow, more skilled
If not more lucky, adroit
To play at the same time with Father, Mother,
Neighbors of small or no regard,
The Mailman even (small-pipped cards
In desultory trade).

At ten engage the friend . . . And then
Twenty-point Aces, Jacks, Queens, Kings
Discard to the grasping Parents, anything
Will buy their leave to flee
To the house in the ox-heart cherry tree
Where waits our dear opponent.
Plank floor and sides and canvas roof,
Airless, uncomfortable, ours . . . There
Through the long hot summer day we play,
Play endlessly, only with him.
Chaste, for no tangible stakes,
We play for the game's, for the endless talking's sake.
Tree blooms, and we, between deals, gather
Short and woody-stemmed bouquets.
Cherries ripe, we stuff our cheeks.
Wasps on fallen cherries bite our feet.
And still we climb to the tree hut where
The game goes on. We measure time by hands,
Shuffle two packs into one
So the deep hot days may last, last long . . .
And they do last
Till they're ambered in memory as happiness.
And then, very suddenly, end.
For dear opponent, almost partner, friend
Grows up, goes off, deserts both game and us . . .
And sets a pattern for all friends.

Ten mopes, but ten recovers soon.
Enters other games, kibitzes more.
Outlandish, passionate variations learns
And swagger stakes plays for . . .
And twenty, thirty, forty turns.

And now our virtuoso hands
Flick the bright cards to mounting piles
For mailman, husband, child.
Late games that strain our best attention,
Crowd our room.
Yet still, there on the window-seat
Where the casement's opened out
And the cherry tree looms dark and green,
We keep two card packs shuffled into one.
And when a friend, rarely these days,
Sits him down and cuts and deals,
Come, smiling at us, Come;
We leave our others to their own resorts
And join him.
Summer is out there.
The great tree wafts kind shawls of wind.
Tree blooms, bears fruit and the dark fruit falls.
But fast, fast now . . . Despite chicane,
Time's measurement remains
An afternoon, a gossipy hand or two.
And then friend goes, goes again, as always.
Smiles, Would you like the casement closed?
Our dear opponent, almost partner goes . . .

With mailman, husband, child we will, must
Play to our wits' to our life's end.
Once lay the cards down with the friend,
There's no more dealing then.

PANDORA—'65

They had been racketing around
Long enough, certainly—
Knocking, coughing falsely, whispering
Followed by uproarious laughter—bum jokes, doubtless.
So finally she pulls out the toy box
And lifts the lid;
Regards with anxious pleasure
As, really remarkably agile
Given the years they've been locked up,
They clamber out and mill around her.

Darkling now, now radiant,
And quaintly costumed—circa nineteen-thirty—
They light her room as windowed figures
Light a church—chapelle jeunesse.
And, like old saints, each one holds
His emblem, aide-mémoire,
Cradled between hand and elbow—
A Mercedes, the Loire, a blue canoe . . .
Very small and wonderfully clear
(As if her glasses were on backwards)
The figures crowd, then part to show
A once familiar face or gesture.

How few the names remembered.

All young, all 'perfectly handsome,'
All taking off for elsewhere, asking,
Will you come? or, Shall I find you
Later? Moments of invitation.

Where did we think we'd go, my darlings?
We inescapably, forever There.

They paw the ground, but forward-back
Like eager ponies disciplined
To gates, like dancers making ready.

>The gates were never swung, the dance
>Did not begin. We learned our brother
>Peer Gynt's lesson—went around
>And came out on the other side,
>Much changed.

Harlequins with cubed guitars,
Carafes and balconies,
The figures merge and separate.
Perspectives of delight.
The woman nods and smiles, affirmative
Of true loves, friendships, conversations.

>How gay, how brave, how promising—
>Surely, blonde back then, 's myself,
>A book in hand . . . And that girl there,
>How prettily she danced the Charleston.

Then skin-sloughed recollection rears explicit
And old-time cinemas replace perception—
Scenes of betrothal, scenes of betrayal,
Sound-track by logomaniacs.

>O my poor dolls! My surrogates!
>How vain, how arrogant, how fearful—

The worn films spit and flick.
The air's obscured by smoky wafts of guilt.

Did we ever help each other?

Long-faced Pinocchios,
They cling about her knees.
And she, hand half-stretched to touch their heads,
Knows she ought to question, make some use of them.
Instead, in new chicane

(Who says A says B)

She shakes them off and rummages
A pile of costumes heaped beside her.
And pell-mell tosses paunches, balding
Heads, divorces, grey curls out among them;
Tosses break-downs, failures, high careers
And disappointments, steadfastness;
Along with a quantity of ordinary
Dresses, suits with masks to match
Of quiet and unquiet desperation.

Caught as caught could,
They patiently exchange
Till each is fitted with his present.

The woman sits back tired, half-ashamed.
Then, moved by the youthfulness that glows
Like light beneath a well-locked door
Along the edges of their bleak disguises,
She kindly indicates the toy box
And stands to bow them in.

She bows her to an empty room,
Or cleared at least. For rustling dresses,
Tactful whispers, commemorative sighs
From low-eaved corners, looking-glass and closet
State they've not gone far.

Yet far enough and quiet to inspect
What she's just glimpsed within the box—
Sound sound asleep, knees bunched,
Grasping tight a toy spade
And puff hair capped about his head—
Half baby and half boy.

Not vanity nor jigging memories
Inform her smile, but deep and joyous
Complicity (the same da Vinci drew)
With this first love, first comrade,
Fellow solipsist.

> Untarnished Aspirants in minuscule,
> With what grave diligence
> We labored in our sand-pile.

Intent to keep his peace,
She kneels, still smiling, down before the box,
Makes mention of his well-remembered name,
And softly shuts the lid.

FUNNY DOINGS

It's some time ago now
That Love walked off
And simply didn't come back.
The neighbors say,
No matter what you do
Or what you don't
That's normal cat behavior.
Though nothing, of course,
Is changed by his departure,
I sometimes miss him.
In fact, (when I take time
To think of it)
I find his disappearance
Oddly disturbing.
It somehow brings to mind
The way my jacket
Slipped through that hole in its pocket
And also vanished.

NOW PLUS THEN

No birds, people or other diversions
Brighten this banal winter
Day we grudgingly inspect.
The tree is bare, the garden ruinous.
Too long, too often looked at our
Desirable estate's got pretty shabby.

And now, as if a clever camera
Man had placed an old old slide
Out there, the scene's in duplicate.
Past radiance matches present gloom
With exactitude of twig for twig,
Not one askew to fault the contrast.

Not one. Yet gaudy hope matched twig
For twig with present un-hope, Love
With Love-forgot fuse to single,
Hard, much clearer images . . .
In bevelled glass, our winter tree
Stands black and bare and fine to see.

THE LIFE OF ACTION

Busy as dwarves,
Presumptive Ganymedes,
Our two boys swarm
Hither and far a-field.
Hurry's the word and Run
That a dozen tasks get on,
That not a one.
Their means are common—
Push and Pull;
Their ends unknowable.
For that hilarious youth,
Their master, perched on the oak
Bough, curved hands at mouth,
Constantly changes their goals.
Yet still commands them, Go,
Little varlets, go, go, go.

Our great Montaigne confessed
He'd bite his tongue, his fingers eating.
Not from greed this haste
But that he had such madness in his feet,
"Quick-silver, maybe," sit-still seemed a waste.
And time pressed.

Montaigne, small boys are immortal.
But even a transient dame—
Mid twentieth century—
Can wake to urgency,
As if today were not the same.
Despite all mirrors, vernal;
Go, go, go informs her.
Go in jubilance, my dame, in laughter.

EXPLICATION DE TEXTE

His shovel and hoe, his balanced fork
Hang sharp and bright by uncle Ned's;
    Now other men
    Are come to heft them,
Dig and delve at his dear work.

How will they do? How will they follow
This line that glimmers into night?
    His tools from dust
    Will drift to rust
With him not here to mark the furrow.

Shovel and fork are sharp and shined,
The furrow's lips a mask of flowers.
    Their satins hide
    The dark divide
Where late the master trued his line.

COME AND GONE

Air even is frozen
To expecting, receiving.
For the whole bush quivered
And one clear note,
Soft as an autumn bird's
Through tough old leaves,
Has reached this alertest huntsman.

Dead-pan, perfectly still,
Prick-ears, prick-mind attendant
On the cat-track spoor
Of syllables that threads
His thought, huntsman awaits
The few more notes he needs
To graph a constellation.

His left hand lifts mid-air
And plucks (alack, good hand,
Too soon, too soon) at silence;
Falters there and falls.
Whereat reception dulls,
Expectance melts away,
The air turns ordinary.

Ordinary, too,
Who strikes a match, pats cat,
Opens a book or other.

IN PRAISE

Silk without weight; liquid without wet;
Caressive yet impalpable.
Trees waving stir what sun has warmed.

We cannot use it as the birds do—
Three swifts quartering the evening sky,
The glider hawk that, quiet, quiets all.

At home though. Like silent fish
Ten fathom down on ocean's pasturage,
We move around each other separately;

Encased, enthralled and gentled by
Our kindest element, the summer air.

FAIR FALLEN

Yes, the soldier said, flicking
A snapshot, we had one like that.
Grandfather's darling (the same
Grave beauty) and the old man his.

Ourselves more hip, like careless brothers
Watched the youngster cut and run,
His face a-blaze, to those indulgent
Arms outstretched for him, and Yelled.

But favorites cannot take it slow.
That strong old man fetched him up
To his saddle-bow and cantered off;
While we, their derelicts, saluted.

A MERRY MEETING

Allemagna? She offers the store with the candy.
He reaches and, Ah! *Allemagna* has recognized.
And how deeply, magnificently blue the sky
Is over Milano, Via Manzoni.

And they are hand in hand, laughing like lovers.
Cinema handsome, they laugh, peering through louvers
At those sleek seals, the Milanese,
Balancing circus-colored cakes and candies.

Leaves pattern plaster—Via Marco di Marchi.
Then he, with affectionate ado,
Goes back to his Piétà, she to the zoo.
Great Milano—villaged by her stranieri.

He takes a sweet and clapboards close around
Them once again—they somewhat breath-bound
Still from when they wandered Milano together
For thirty seconds, and were lovers.

SNOW-WHITE AND ROSE-RED

That last time, too, our talk was flowers—
    My special roses, white
And red and side by side, slightly
    Apart from the others.

I get it, she laughed, I understand.
    Our fingers met as absence
Cleared—we strolling from the present
    Back to our fairy-lands.

Today, a lasting absence has closed
    Round her. And not a soul
Is left to comrade me that stroll
    Or read old tales in roses.

MOURNING AS MAKING

Back there when the earth was flat
And always, so it seems, snow-covered,
When the fabulous cities were merely lights
Along the edge, in no way dazzling;
Out of the chimney of some snow-mounded
Dwelling on the plain we'd sometimes see
A darkling, twisted flame emerge
And twisting wind, rich in rich colors,
Up into the deep and starless sky.
We'd follow its ascent and wish it well.
Then, through many days, our old folk
Waxed prolix. They who had known
That soul as ordinary, like themselves—
O, it's life's the leveller—would recall
Its habits, its particularities,
Its manner of being kind or stern
Until, unique, never to be repeated
Or replaced, they'd readied it in its own
Dress for the brilliant company of death.

"Sit down, my dear," the great-aunts welcomed me,
"We're mourning for your grandmother."
Often those ladies wept; often,
Festive in re-creation, laughed very gaily.

DA MING

(The Shining People)

1

To visit their dear Ming-children's tombs
The bright-robed gods, their lotus fingers
Rock to rock, loiter down
The chasmed hills that rim the plain.

Men must use the Spirits' Walk,
Dusty and flat, fantastically
Guarded, right and left, by carved stone
Camels, unicorns and dragons,
Elephants—some eighteen pair.
Huge, that no leaf shadows
Mitigate, weather-beaten
Grey they rear against the hills,
The grey, grey-green and tawny hills.
And where they once brayed, bleated,
Trumpeted affirmatives
Now silence roves . . . Austere pleasaunce.

2

Enstoned affirmatives provide
Both sights to see and picnic spots . . .
Thus, some sixty years ago,
Complete with donkeys, paniers, drivers,
A happy bridal pair arrives
To view the imperial grave-yard.

Five thousand miles of land and sea
They've travelled; he on his country's business,
She on his. His naval whites
Topped by two gold bars announce
His competence, a twenty waist-
Band hers. Out on the coast, gun-boat

With stripèd flag enlists their duty.
Today they're free to tourist it.

Her ruffled skirt, her parasol
Make patterns in the ancient dust
As arm in arm they pass beneath
The slender gates and brave the alley;
Talking aloud of emperors
And animals, but with their eyes
Of youth and love. Immortal pair!
Safe past the watchful camels' malice,
They stop at six great elephants,
Benign as life, that seem to sway
A little even . . . The guide book says
To throw a stone upon one's back
For luck. She picks the stone, he throws.
Stone stays and luck is theirs—as if
They hadn't known . . . And quickly passing
Other wardens reach their goal,
"Full of grand quiet and reserve."
The words, the sight are sobering.

Who as princelings just now paced
Their flowery realm are brought up short
By marble balustrades in tiers,
Red lacquer columns, double roof
Of tile like bamboo rods and vari-
colored as the hills behind,
The corners tilted. Clearly a temple;
Yet, so spread, as clearly house.
They grope their whole inheritance
To buy excursion tickets there;
And find debased and meagre cash
Of half-recalled, machine-cut Gothic.
Jingle it may, but not buy this.
Nor does their modest Pantheon

Afford them precedent for what
Celestial assemblies meet
Herein, for what convivial;
When spirits of thirteen emperors,
Fathers-sons whom death has brothered
(Although Yung-Lo who built Peking
Is still the eldest) entertain
The saffron-robed, the lotus-fingered
Gods, their fathers.
                    A deferential
Pause—our young ones face about.
They're disappointed with the Ming;
Also, good children, with themselves.
That's hard to bear. How happy then
To greet their comfortable friends,
The elephants, and toss off guilt
As earlier they tossed a stone.
Royal again and hand in hand,
They laugh for pleasure in their camp
Of flop-eared donkeys winningly
Alive, of whipping pig-tails where
Descendants of the Ming brew tea
And smile and bow and welcome them.

3
Count now, count—for twenty waist's
Broke thirty; slim gold bars have swelled
To admiral's galloons. She
Competent for family, he
For squadrons (good children make good rulers)
These two have picnicked, land and sea,
The world's admired spots (amassed
No little wealth, as tourists go)
Enjoyed their lives, admit no lack
Excepting immortality.
Youth's fled to slimmer waists and bars.

Love like a Colorado river's
Dug so deep between them, neither
Dare look for it . . . Count now, count
The years since they have laughed together;
Years when, phrased for semaphore,
Official courtesies alone
Have crossed the chasmed living-room.
Count the decades lived by rule.

So holidays are welcome—Christmas,
Easter—when children's agile leaps
From side to side obscure the chasm;
Their merry-making drowns the silence.
Playing games on such a day,
One child teases, Tell me, father—
Mother, if not yourselves what bird
Or animal you'd choose to be.

As with one voice, they reply,
An elephant.
                    The children die
At such incongruous agreement.
The parents smile, yet do not speak
Nor search each others' eyes. Shawled
In the quaint decorum of the old,
Rheumatic fingers laced, they raise
Their heads and look far far away.

Evening is falling slow across
The China plain. In mildest light
A lacquer-columned, temple-palace
Lifts and spreads its lucid beauty.
And listening ears can catch now leafy
Rustlings as the saffron-robed,
The smiling gods stroll down the hills
To grace their childrens' party.

DECEMBER

O mama, mama, mama—
              how sailorly
You plied the archipelagoes;
From stove to roses, books to child!
Then, hale matron, sound as your own Rome apples,
Through endless-seeming, Gothic-coloured autumns
Shared their ripeness.
            Both now distillates,
The one Rome left's a blob among bare boughs
And you are bird-boned, grey and small.

I loiter by the fence, admiring
Bare boughs against a white stone sky,
Long-eared await the quiet fall
Of dark seed onto dark earth.

Upstairs, blob and boughs configurate
White walls where the old woman,
Tired suddenly, has lain her down.
She lies wide-eyed—as when a child that's idling
Out a summer day holds still to watch
The shapes of sparrows flock through shapes of leaves—
Her face tranquil in entire attention.
And I, her birdy-hand in mine, am tranquil.

Mama, there are not many days now
Till the end of the year,
But the minutes are bountiful.

A GUIDED TOUR

(*Introduction for a Posthumous Book of Verse*)

If you'd come sooner, ladies-gentlemen,
Not today especially but years,
You might have seen

        with rosy heels
        And heavy hair flop-hatted

Her running from the pond down there or walking
Carefully, carefully in her net carrying
Gold fish and black, fan-tails, shiners.

        These are my thoughts, she used to say,
        Laughing as loving at us lunk-heads,
        What I could catch of them.
        And I must house them well.

She'd then spend days arranging weeds
And tunnelled rocks for them to swim through,
Adjusting lights and jets of water.
And though we thought she overspent
Her youth and strength to shift one rock
From here to there to back again,
When we couldn't see the slightest difference,
We did find her aquariums
Remarkable. So dark, so bright—
The fish so quick and various.

        What are they for? she'd laugh at us,
        That's up to you.

She pays them no mind now,
Nor looks for fish now;
But sits there by the pond,
Crouched who used to run;
And vague who was intense;
A statued mist.
Long grass has grown up through her net
And maiden pinks crowd round the floppy hat.
Sometimes an old carp surfaces
And blows companionable bubbles to her.
Perhaps they chat.

    Now bluest water's merely glass
    To saffron willow-weed.
    Swallows diving punctuate
    Our speech, but they don't speak.
    Any day now, carp and she'll be gone
    And Lord, how mournful then our pond.

In this room here's her old, her youthful work.

    Things not looked at fade, she used to say.

Ladies and gentlemen, please come
This way—and look at her aquariums.

FROM

A PENITENTIAL
PRIMER

JUBILANCE

The white mule trotted out of the dooryard
between the flowering Judas and the dogwood trees.
And the black men trotted gaily after it,
keeping well behind and laughing, as if for years
they'd said their useful mule would fly the coop.
White mule, white mule—hey, fella, you—
come back, white mule. They made out to catch
       while their calling
followed like going along with the mule, like
       pleasure
in the red road beyond the bend.

The pink child laughed at the men and the mule
and claimed it never did come back,
said not in the daytime nor at night
did any black man ride the white mule home.
White mule, white mule, they may have called,
You fella, hey, come back—like singing in the dooryards.
Admiring and laughing, as if of themselves they sang
of a useful mule that showed much wit
and clipped the road on hard as ivory feet.

LUXURY

When the renounced lover reappears
in well known suit and face familiar,
It's only a dream, the Self repeats
and hides behind the mask of sleep
that deceives no one. Like a Venetian lady,
idle and wilful, the Self would dally.
Would believe the obstinate old rowboat
lust a prowed gondola and float
in dreamy-sweet and billowy inconsequence
to just one more seduction. Innocence
itself her face, she delicately prances
to the reiterated invitation of Africk dances.

Though mask and Venice fade, the rowboat
perseveres against the waking hours.

NEPENTHE

And sometimes drugged and visionary love
projects beyond the boundaries of fact,
as dearly waded brooks spring-drunk
can brim their pastures' stoniest denials.
And those two great gray figures
often seen at dawn half-sitting
half-reclining on a tumbled bed,
their legs still negligently interlaced,
those no-eyed granite gods, pause
a longer more reflective moment
and hear beyond their thin fantastic hearts.
Profoundest pause, as if young men could live
to learn croquet and watch their daughters' daughters
dance in flowery cities sheltered by those thighs.

POVERTY

Our little sister used to write us wonderful letters
that the Monsignor would quote at missions.
And she sent us remarkable testimonials
from superior and wealthy families who wished she were
                                        still in their service.

We always imagined a bright flower on her kitchen sill
and that she sanded an oak table,
sang by an open fire
and prepared wholesome food for all those friends of hers.

Most interesting gifted and worthwhile friends they were,
working men, artists, philosophers,
any saint you could mention
who asked nothing better than to sit in her kitchen—
                                        or so she wrote.

Awhile back her letters stopped. Then the newspapers
and other reliable sources
spread tales about her.
So we went to see for ourselves what had happened.

We looked through the window
and saw her lolling in a low chair like a bad woman,
or a mother nursing—
saw her this way and that through the gaps in the great
                                        crowd.

She looked peakèd and old and miserable like a bad woman,
she looked stern and tender and patient like a good mother;
and we'd never have recognized the delicate girl of the letters
at all, except that we noticed a rusty geranium.

50

All the people were asking her to go somewhere else—
either so they could kill her
or so they could tidy the room.
Every so often one of them grabbed up a child
(there were lots around, some beautiful,
some shrivelled as if from rat-bites)
and shook it close to her face, then let it go and went on
                                        talking.

Our little sister bounced one toe against the rickety table leg
and smiled beyond them all,
smiled way beyond their shouting faces
as if to tell somebody far off that she was staying, no
                                        matter what.
Suddenly the commotion stopped and she sat alone
carelessly petting the children,
both shrivelled and beauties.
And we saw that all the time a man'd been standing by the
                                        coal oil stove.

He wasn't at all a remarkable man,
yet we've never forgotten his face.
He didn't speak to her or pay her any mind,
just stood around as if he'd married her
and accepted everything about her a long time ago.
His fingers worked on some small repair job—
or it could have been handcuffs that kept his wrists so close—
but he wasn't struggling,
he wasn't submissive.
He accepted.

The Monsignor says that all we saw was the Devil's lie,
that only the letters are true.
We should have questioned the man.
It's been a number of years now since the Monsignor saw
                                        our little sister.

QUIET

On grey days we look down for light,
down where rainy leaves lie bright
as winking ashes. And to left and right
the trees shine. Red leaves fall soon
but yellow make a radiant noon
of dusk, so close to hand we soon
see nothing else. The grey sky
skimming with threats, the crow's cry
remove into an outside outdoors sky.
Winnowed through these insubstantial walls,
strangers or friends, the dark material
husks of men flit by without footfall.
And our dear ghosts sift softly through the leaves
to laugh and chat here, they and we half mist half
trunks of trees.

RESIGNATION

Clings to the cold rim of the pot,
head bowed and eyes tight shut—
mat spot of cloth and hair
crouched beneath the porcelain walls—
and wails, O mother where's
my warmth, my kind delight, my dream?

Mother smiles complacently and starts
recital of the grown-up part;
then bite-lip bends, fingers weaving
veils of hair to hide her grieving.
Frail arms stretch to strong. Crouched
beneath the wrong that's done them, son
and mother cling to affection's
rim and weep together.

TINTAGEL

Up from anonymous sleep, up
through lightening waves of revery,
aware of blurred limbs casually stirring
that were their taut life line and plummet
through the maelstrom, with what serenity
the hardy divers make their slow way up
to room and furniture and discarded clothing.

Eyes perceive a known pair of eyes,
greet the resurgent self, and gratitude
inspires the personal protective gesture,
half-humorous embrace, the domesticity
of flesh that's wonder to such as lately dived
through green green cyclones of the sea.

But his meditative finger pauses
on her breast, her moving lips are mute.
They note their aptitude for gestures
used before and sweetly with another.
In double image both corrupt, belovèd
and deceived present their mingled breasts,
belovèd and deceived lend ear to frozen lips.

Green tides report a wisdom to their bones.
They separate and clothe their nakedness.
He on a chair, she upright on the couch,
like neighborly hermits they explore
their selves and exorcise the flesh and memory.

"I'm hungry and there's nothing here to eat,"
he says; and she, "The children will be home."
As tender brothers part who'll meet tomorrow,
they wash and dress and lock the door together.
Princely their progress down the rosy street,
and from their gait and from their eyes such
                              mildness flows
a threadbare populace is fed and clothed.

UNDERSTANDING

When the vacuum filled on the rooftree
like a smokeless powder factory
exploding, I choked on my throat
while the child sat still between afraid and not.
So, swallowing, "That old Mr. Thunder
certainly is bustling his furniture
around," I said
and almost added,
"Honey." I spoke authentically
in the voice of an early
nurse of my own, of the good
nurse of all times, everywhere,
of the kind person, the interpreter.

FROM

VILLA NARCISSE

TO THE PATRON

On this staled stretch of beach,
    The double fork
As long as some men's sunny shadows reach,
    Its curving fingers worked
Round emptiness, arms closed or manacled;
    The tender knife,
Blunt blade and heavy heft, in half a life-
    Time's blowing sands half-held
    Are useless artifacts
    Of a mis-adventurer,
    A lonely mariner,
        North-tossed, storm-wracked.

Yet I've heard tell, Below
    This bitter gray
Lie waters mild and blue that lip the low
    Lain lands to sunny bays.
And happy boatmen singing sail and plunder
    Them—arms wide
And plunged their curious fingers over boatside—
    Of salt-encrusted wonders.
    And the glad knife leaps
    In hard and skilful palms
    To work the watery farms
    Of Chesapeake.

Master, sweet gentleman,
    Subscribe my voyage.
Take some stock in those exacter lands
    And in my mute tools' rage
For use. Profit by my indenture there.
    Thou needst not go
Nor new ship lend. Search what imperfect, shallow

To the Patron

     Vessel needs repair;
     A-leak, with ragged sheets
     And stripped of parts, no ship,
     That now drifts derelict
        Beyond belief.

A DREAM

Was chatting with the French girl there
in the bright pine room of faceless people
all familiar. Saw her then
instructing him—him avid, eager—
in deceit. Saw the weary
weight of his desire on her.
"Cover the left page when she reads,"
and raised their guilty eyes to me.

And so betrayal's blackjack socks
the heart, and so of it the horror . . .
While one of all that chittering bird-like
crew and those impassive two
had glasses thick enough to see
not me but bull-dumb raging sorrow
swaying there and led me to
an empty room and closed the door.

Although we woke at ease and no
French girl has been and the days pass;
the horror stays and under it
the dream-learned, dream-pervasive sorrow.
And rooms are empty where I sit
admiring my super-subtle self
that did its true, its onelie love
traduce and murder while he slept.

WHAT WORLD WELL LOST?

How small the world! Thus two, in wide disdain
    Remark where Norumbega's
Shrunk from a continent and mountain chain
        To a Charles' side
        Canoe ride.

No Ralegh he nor she no Pembroke's countess,
    Boarding their fragile shallop
Search, with fifty others, privateness
        On the rushy bay
        One mile each way.

From crowded scene, precisely irised eyes
    Observe each other, part,
Return by chance and there surprised, collide
        To a deepening stare.
        While here and there

His paddle parts the water, waterly moments
    Softly flow and luminous
As, following eyes, their hearts like continents
        Grow large and merge,
        Strain to the verge

Of the orbed world. Far voyage! Breasts
    A-burst with magnanimity
Scatter extra beauties over the least
        Bull-rush and wavelet,
        Invest the sun-lit

Marsh with golden castles, rivers open-mouthed
    With gold from Norumbega
Canoed with plumed caciques, parrots, pards and all South
      Born imaginings
      To Northern princelings.

Intrepid captains of the quivering air,
    Masters of fabled wealth,
They promise at the next bend to declare
      And take possession
      Of their passion;

Place standards, kneel and voice exultation.
    When a common radio song
Cuts the taut chord in common proclamation
      Of disenchantment.
      The gold element

Turns rusty. Eyes retract and hearts retreat
    To former latitudes.
And back to doom of home his paddle beats
      Their agony for all
      That's safe and small.

And should they later bless or curse the song
    Who, hearing, smile and let
Rememberance of wonder ease the wrong
      Of dream fordone
      And a neat horizon?

Great-visioned Ralegh also turned him back
    Before the last bend
To the angry queen, as knowing who gold lack
      Must guilt her knife
      With all his life.

In the strait tower waiting, no bird-
    Song broke upon his writing
But ballat like Greensleves. And, as he heard,
      He leaped the span
      Of youthful ocean

And tumbled where his mutinous sailors sang
    To slake their loneliness
And slackened him while the dead-pan caciques rang
      Their changes on his eager-
      ness for Norumbega,

The two-edged commonness that cuts our ears
    From truth to harvest solace.
Towered Ralegh, deaf now, glossed the years,
      Exacted revenge,
      Accomplished the bend.

FIVE VALENTINES FOR ONE

Thou whittles to the core of *you*,
Communal, custom-blunt, diffuse.
Thou is a foreign single use
Like Love that talks so foreign through
Our native words and bends us to
Perceive them singular, as old views
Seen by travellors turn new.
Thou is a sweet-belled jester's shoe
That trips us back past centuries
Of ash to Tuesday carnivals
And hopeful, dream-hatched memories.
So I'll be-thou thee, love, and shall
Reach nearer thee by strange address,
Like old plays, than by commonness.

You love by habit now, they jeer.
Yes, as I dress myself I may
Put on an Irritance or Calm, play-
Shorts of Busyness or sheer
Affection's dancing dress. I wear
My Duty's close-cut pants or gay
Maternal skirts, make bold display
Of patched Indifference. These mere
And daily habits circumvent
By novelty and play of pride
My mild ingenuous body's constant
Willingness to lay aside
Such masks, its barefaced wish for thee
To cover and inhabit me.

I pity women matched to men,
Men good and gifted who great-bellied
Pant and heave and lurch their stolid
Witless, untaught, muscle-frozen
Flesh. Reluctant Leda's friend
So subtly web-stepped his invalid
Arguments that hot for gelid
Wings she ran to him. Mock-solemn
As the rose flamingoes dance
Desire and pattern it, my own
Most simple human love can prance—
With smile a tombed Etruscan loaned—
A mime enchanting as when gnomic
Eros schooled his frantic Psyche.

I dreamed thou gav'st my corpse to curious
Doctors, fit end for prisoners,
Who looked in vain for failures' years'
And sorrows' chains and for their infamous
Gangrene. But they did find, most marvelous,
Nerves and muscles, ducts for tears
And bile with golden wires geared.
Then argued they if Paracelsus
Changed my chains, or Faustus ran
Their heaviness to fluent strength,
Rehearsed deluded charlatans
Of myth and fact at learnèd length.
Mere quacks themselves whose learning missed
The fierce chief of alchemists.

Public brutality and private
Pain are all, they say, that's left
With God and Love in Limbo. Yet—
As old Ausonius's roses state
Sweetness enought to mitigate
Half Rome; as dreamy monks who wept
For Icarus like prophets kept
Men sleepless for a wingèd fate;
So thou, my singed Icarian,
Dost hide like Cretan catacombs
From scandalized barbarians
One lone man-animal become
As gentle, natural and sane
As roses, bulls or aeroplanes.

AN EVENING OF DEATH

One stone in the boundless ennui of the always
Poor, he drops on the bed, rippling ennui
Over the stove, the chair and Rose his wife,
The starveling oaks beyond the sagging door,
    Over his every day, his life.
        I came for the kitten, Jerdan,
          That you promised me, the white child says;
          The pink and gold and white, the beauty-
          ful child-angel from the mansion house.

He turns away. He has been kind all day,
His work a centre for her lonely play.
He has no more to give, he'd like to get
And curses Rose whose kindness knows no time,
    Who scoops the litter up and says,
        Sit on the steps, chile, and choose your kitty.
        Jerdan tahd, he don' want no play.

The oaks are gathered at the wall's wide cracks
And ennui ripples down the shaft of sun.
They have all the else, Rose, with the poor
One share your timeless kindness, share with me.
    Give, Rose, man's always luxury.
      Rose, Rose, the angel sings,
        Which is the one I want the most?

A-thwart the glare, the softly stepping friend
A-grin and holding out a pint of gin
Appears. O, did he know that I'd be here
Or was the gin for Rose and him? Step past
    The child and shut the door. We'll drink
        While Eeny, meeny, miney, moe,
        Catch a monkey by the toe—
        I'll take the black one, Rose,
        Can he be mine?

Rubs with an alien beat on gin-taut ears.
Hot thought-beasts crackle through the underbrush
Of all their minds and drink at flowing fires.
Rose rocks and smiles. The two men crouch and stare.
    Their razors flare. The door swings wide.
        Now Jerdan isn't tired, Rose,
        He's running fast, he'll catch that man.
        But look, he trod my kitten flat,
        The Blackie that I'd chose.

A leopard strains again in work-dulled limbs
And jungly greenness sways and hums with vein-
Impounded blood. And he will catch the man.
His deeply sharpened knife will teach him not
    No more to gin up Rose his wife.
        Yet scrapes a foot along the wire grass;
        Scat, scat, black cat. Why I mus' feel
        Your black fur through my horn-shod heel?

Sudden the dark sky, the churning river.
The other turns and it is his deep knife
Jugs out a life; while Jerdan tries to plug
His leaky throat and bail back in the radiant
    Years to come, the years gone by.
        Black cat, why you stick so fas'?
        For feelin' you, black cat, I los' my trick.
        For the Lord's sake, angels, start
        And sing me out this rack.

After the brief parade, after the torches,
Child and kittens creep from out the bushes
To where the mourning woman sits and rocks
Beside the stone-cold body on the bed.
    Holding the stiffening kitten soft,
        Is Jerdan dead, Rose? asks the child.
    She eyes the quiet bed and spreads
    A meagre bough for Blackie's bier.

He daid, chile, like you say. Jerdan is daid.
(So's my kitty, and weeping winds her in the empty
Arms) He tahd after that 'ere race,
Daid tahd. And so is Rose. Rose feels it's late.
    Choose you a cat and scamper home.
        But I have chose. I chose
        Poor Blackie there and now he's dead.

        Bright angel, keep right on your singing:
        Jerdan and Rose are listening.

THE PARASITE

Thrust through the wild voracious green
Of this famed vine, so rare, so dear.
Beneath magnificence of blooms
and leaves, bird-nests and ropey stems
your hand will find no ruined tree
but human beings stifled here.
Two skeletons the stanchion make
that holds the vine that is their tomb.
It first devoured, now decorates.

Long ago, these two were busy
like the others in the wood,
at ease with them and ordinary;
When they chanced upon a little
root, unnamed, unknown, but orris
sweet, like Grecian moly that
preserved a man from swinishness.
Take it, the others said, we know
it costly, scant, of high repute
though we forget just why. We know
it must not be allowed to die.
Will you not rear it with us then?
No, no. We lack both time and strength.
Our daily habits and desires
use all our efforts. You go plant
your pretty root and see what it
will do. Mocking and truthful, they
refused to trifle with the thing.

But these two carried it in hope
and tenderness to this cleared space.
Just by this little bit removed
them from the gloomy peopled wood
to give their fondling sun and room.
And its care bound them close, let them
forget the mocking multitude.

Soon their root was happy there
and grew and bloomed in works and days.
Proudly then they sent out children,
bearing and wreathed in greenery,
as witness to their good, to tell
how flowered, tendrilled, beautiful
the root had grown. As joyful
invitations they were sent and
were appeals for help, though these
two unaware they needed it.
But none asked where the vine had grown.
None followed from the children to
the clearing where these waiting stood.
And if their children prospered in
the wood, they never knew. For now
their ankles so entwinèd were
in their dear work they durst not move.

Hands on each other's trembling shoulders,
as they at first in awe had gazed
into each other's eyes, they now
in terror looked and drowned there still
but found no worlds, no promises.
Depth upon depth of loneliness
they saw and recognized. And while
they gazed, the vine's green fire leaped
aloft and prisoned them entire.

Say that they thought this root might be
a transient gourd to shelter them,
say that at most they hoped to grow
a tree of shade for weary friends,
say they mistook the climate, age:
These say love garrotes its host.

M'S STORY

On a pretty day for conversation
And a stroll, a halcyon
Of azure fall,

Blonde Ann bestrode her 'miscellaneous
Pleasure horse' while Victor vigorous
Walked and tall.

On his left hand, a bird at hover
Was hardly stayed by the careful cover
His right lent.

said Ann: Say Life's a horse, I ride light-reined.
and he: My bird sings best when least restrained.
And both were silent.

then A: Sometimes the horse decides the pace.
and V: Smallest birds demand great space
And variety.

A: They say that confidence and balance
Will see you safe through maverick dance
Or ferocity.

V: With strength and care my faltering hands
Make perch and cage so bird may stand,
Or sit and carve

His wings . . . Their gaily way led through
Alfalfa fields of twinèd blue.
View slant, view far

From her high seat Ann wonders found,
While different wonders Victor's down-
    Cast eyes discerned.

So it was like a thing to tell
Her of—how suddenly she fell.
    Bright hair has burned

The blue lucerne, was his first cry.
How long will you thus broke-necked lie?
    He scolded her.

For all your proud and pretty comment,
Ann, were you unconfident?
    Unbalanced were

You just the little minute needed
To undo you? She seemed to heed
    Though not reply.

Your horse turns huge on the horizon—
Then saw his care-less hands and groaned.
    Huge and high,

Unfaltering, a buzzard cruised,
Corruption lifting to the blue
    The stainless sky.

FAR SOUTH

Virtuous apples fairy dragons
Ought to guard, the grape-fruit fall
    On plain green grass. Among

Their branches perch the commonest birds,
The red, the mocking and the long-legg'd
    Black that shake the trees.

All singing. Canopies of singing
Net the leaves. Song bubbles fall
    On grass among gold apples.

I'd like to walk over the green river
And chat with my friends there in the trees,
    Play catch with their gold balls

And hear their yearly music patter
Grass. But I am grown into
    A strange and tourist class

That makes the birds grow still and hide.
My nurses are afraid of me,
    They know I'm not a child.

Grown up to exile, I remain
This side the flowing green and watch,
    Without touch or smell or smile

The yellow grape-fruit fall while birds,
The red, the mocking and the long-legg'd
    Gentle-handed black

Make of my childhood's plain and gay
Reality improbable,
    Defenceless fairy tales.

FLIGHT SOUTH

The Lord outdid himself that day
The grackles landed,
Crackling disbanded
Over the elm and fixed
Themselves like tarry irridescent flowers
On its bare sticks;
There squeaked and called for hours
Till off for Washington's
Sargasso islands.
Maintaining elm shape in their going,
They seemed a black-bespangled parachute,
Wind-loosed,
Southward floating.
O, fine to see. But still more wondrous—
O, then seemed Lord-miraculous—
That broad-beamed
Dapper dame
Who kirtled her skirt and ran with them
From street side to back hedge,
Stood there, arms spread,
As balanced on the edge
Of mystery
Or azure sea.
She stood as she had stood a maid
And run from men
To find her dream of man,
Or as a child she ran
Wind in her mouth
Simply to run.
And always at the hedge,
Last ledge,
Stopped stock.

And then bewildered, smiling, half-ashamed
    Turned back.
  I wondered, does Our Lord make mock
    Who proffers such frail 'chutes
    To get us to our South?
Or did two different miracles together come,
    Of birds and Southern sun
    And of a woman?
  And nothing to do with Him the human
    Enviable heart
    That's ever hedged apart
    And ever once more will run.

FOR MOSES

Beyond the beautiful Marys,
the dazzling young god-bearers,
beyond the miraculous Sarahs and Ste. Annes
who bathed in the back-wash of annunciations,
content that divinity
run in the family;

blessèd are the not-named
mothers, those not claimed
by god or hero, whom we dearly prize,
so nimble, gnarled, like sorrow nearly wise,
in books and pictures;
whom we conjecture

when, not often, sun-set
happens on a quiet
figure rocking bow-backed by the window
dog-work at her feet, all ways as if widowed,
the only grown
up one among

so many many children.
Yes, this quiet woman,
this gentle helper of all helplessness
brought forth to care for, glory-less
to serve small things
and guard growing.

Servant or guardian,
 servant or gardener,
mother or nurse, the back bows the same,
hands callous and the figure rocks and dreams
        in the brief rest
        time of sun-set.

So, when the tug shoved off
 and left me on the wharf
who'd run so very fast to go to Norfolk,
the lady my mother over the widening water,
        Moses, cried,
        mind that child.

Fetched him round quick
 and stern then from his gossip.
"Why for you here? your hair oncomb
an' a muddy face. You come along home."
        Through cranes and rails,
        wailing like Israel,

yet tight to his hand holding I trotted, yanked and scolded,
"Deed an w'en figs is des dis minit bus"
an' at they sweetes' and the big city dream loss solaced
        by fruitful earth-
        love from him whom no birth

of any sort ennobled
 but whom care enabled.
Yes, care for and a poor man's merely to live
care enable unslaked longing to perceive
        in Moses an other
        mirage of mother.

AT NIGHT ALL CATS ARE GRAY

Out of the high-noon sun of power
And clemency that grown-ups shed,
And where no shadows are,
The child awakes to find the day
Half done and shadows everywhere.
They trail the regal suns like veils
And longer, longer grow until they merge.

Now grave now gossipy, small pink
And giant black reviewed the ways
Of God and onion sets.
While roosters cock-a-doodled spring
They hitched their boxes close along
The rows, limpid lake to rock-face
Smiling; gnarled hand circling tender, teaching.

Now he's trapped a rat and, swinging
From his other hand, she's pleaded,
Hoped and joked for dear life
To the laundry . . . But, bruise bare toes
Or puny fists, water will mount
And rat climb high and nothing stop
That laughter. Then the rat shrieked, then the child.

Mother! carved in calm, a softness
Lights thy lap, thy thimble flickers
Light birds to the mirror—
Mother! 's sorry . . . The sobbing room
Stands still and taut to dark, of glass
And of a shape down there that carries
Shadows in each hand into the shadows.

BALLET

A miniature audience with mothers
Swarms the tarnished opera house as future
    Ballerinas, six to twelve,
        Observe Giselle,
    The inspired dancer, leste Giselle.

My awkward body, drought-strained eyes can learn,
Can profit from that halt, that carvèd turn,
    That beauty come and gone, that spear
        That gently tears
    The thick old target of my heart.

And thick-fleshed heart's preserved by teary brine.
But for those cardboard, flat, those Valentines—
    Giselle, should your spear be the first
        To tear and hurt
    The pre-virgin, undisturbed?

The child beside me gasps, "I never dreamed,"
Her eyes still on Giselle, "I never dreamed
    That it would be so beautiful."
        How bountiful
    The cry of cardboard heart grown supple

In first blood, blood drawn and fed by carvèd
Turn. For spear so savantly retarded
    Hit its mark and tender targe
        Has swelled too large
    To fit its size. O, far too large.

Ballet

Small hands pat apt applause, yet almost all
the Valentines stayed one-dimensional.
And she so near to me can't tell
If it be well
So young to find celeste Giselle.

TEMPLE

Its charm is delicate and seeps
In a mild radiance through the mind;
The view is housed and kind,
Cloud-streaked
And orchard meek.

The gaudy song-birds do not venture
So far North, but small brown uses
Are catered to by bushes
And the juniper's
Harsh verdure.

Tree though or bush seem always still.
Under the wind that cries in the mountain,
Under the hurt of the plain-
Song whitethroat's shrill,
It's very still.

The place is of women, the long haired women
Of family who make bread and sew,
Who roses tend and throw
Doors open
For the children:

And gossip at dusk with their murdered men-folk
Gathered beneath the great-boled ash.
Passions run grey as glass,
As smooth, engross
Both hosts and ghosts.

Temple

Time even is womaned, circular,
Anarchic. Sleep finds out the children
 Stretched like careful herdsmen
  Of the stars;
  While books of old wars

Absorb the mothers' faint remorse
For privateness. Long hair a-stream,
 Over late fires they dream
  Of lives lost
  Well, of heroes.

AFTER THE LATE LYNCHING

No,
It goes not liquidly for any of us.
    Yseult
      's as hard as Troilus.
    Heloise is far away and
      Difficult.
    Nor's Death felicitous.
    Not princes' proud defiant trumpets,
      Not good men's easyness
      With Death is not ours yet

Whose lives construe so little of what is brave.
    Grace notes
    Should not be asked of slaves.
    Slaves' is, lunk-dumb and mutinous,
      At whipping posts
    To crouch and whine till they've
Spelled out the primitive construction—
    So plain, so difficult—
    Of a death and a woman.

Nor not from whitest light of foreign poems
    Hope help;
    But from her native woe
    Who took that black head in her hands
      And felt,
    "A sack of little bones";
    Whose arms for the last time round him knew,
    "All down one side no ribs
    But broken things that moved."

HOW GENEROUS!

How generous are the poor
In things!
Their sagging door
's a-swing—
Shove in, son—to any poorer yet.

"So may my children knocking find
A door unlocked
and kind-
ness when they wander through the world alone."

Who know the delicious meat
Of hunger
Press something to eat
On the stranger
And a present of some sort for the visiting child.

Untaught to usury,
Give on
Borrowed money.
So on,
Flows on sweet charity, unblocked and warm.

Pure of possessions,
Are able
Mathematicians
To label
Most goods X and so deal freely with them.

A VALUE OF MUSIC

And the debased aristocrat hates these,
Her unclassed child's appliances for pleasure:
Boots are inimical to grace and skis,
    Like careless planking leaned a-slant
      The upright, stress its want
Of elegance. Desperately measured
Anguish fills the woman and she weeps.
    Weeps for an enervating strain
    Of boots picked up and dropped again,
The object-weighted sorrows of the weak.

Sturdier flesh of her, less fevered bone,
It is the child that from the upright box
Now plucks such cubes and cylinders and cones
    As Mozart, say, would unify
      Into a parquetry
Or citadel of luminous building blocks.
Self-multiplying quartz refracts all things—
    Boots even—to a first estate,
    Polygonal, patriciate.
The woman is a smile, remembering.

We read how dancing-shoes trip down the stairs
Of history while sabots mount, a theme
For praise. Praise too such ordering of air
    As teaches us to understand
      How astute Talleyrand
Could mourn "the sweetness of the old regime."
We think he did not merely dote, but tried
    To abstract from his memories
    Of Trianon and Tuileries
A quartz climate and a passionate child.

THE SISTERS

Miss America:
> It's autumn now and morning's shortest
shadows stretch like evening's on
the brilliant grass, with fiery phlox
and purple aconite for warmth's
memorials. And still she sat.
A ghost, I hoped, fantastic for
old ease in slat-backed garden chairs.
For though I saw no more than high-heeled
wooden shoes that guarded small,
impractical bare feet and quiet
hands that wreathed her blood-bespattered
hair with phlox and aconite,
I felt her sly blue Renoir
eyes assess my quarter acre
and my Cape Cod house. I hoped
and did not scant my chores. Then smoothed
my pretty apron, smoothed my hair
that's always washed and neat and sat
down opposite. And for a long time
we did not speak while in between us
flowed the years of since I left
our mother's house and she remained;
and settled to the younger sister's
alternating pain of love
and jealousy.
> "Well, miss," she said,
mocking my virginity,
my years of service in new lands.
"Well, miss," as Englishmen say 'miss'
to waitresses, who never did
a lick of work herself but rich
or poor would drip the gold-shot years

between her quiet hands while I
was grabbing minutes. Then kicked her worn
old fish-net bag and tumbled out
her treasures on the grass. "I thought
perhaps your poor sad orphans—", while Chartres,
the Piétà of Avignon,
Mont St. Victor and Pelleas,
Essais, Pasts, Misfortune's Flowers
littered the grass with here and there
a jewel that she used to wear
to balls or country carnivals.

"They're young, you know," I said. "They like
their simpler games, Erector or
Meccano now."
            "And when, in God's name,
when do you propose to let
them grow?" she should have said. But she
had changed and mildly shoved at Chartres
with painted toes. "Perhaps you're right.
They're so disarming in their youngness,
are they not, your funny orphans?
And these don't shine as I remembered.
They're old, of course, and then your air's
so dry." But bright enough to burn
they made a widening scorch upon
my watered green, disturbing me,
so *made* I knew that they must be
corrupt, though no doubt beautiful.
"Well, miss," more gently now, "let's see
your house." And truly marvelled at
my brand-name kitchen. "But what is this?"
Lifting an old-time latch, she found
the ell I'd never got around to
tearing down and never used.
And found my old bed-chamber, angled,

low and bare with white-washed walls
and pallet bed and one straight chair,
Went in and laid her down.
While I must wait outside the door,
too plump to enter it, though I
had slept here all my slim-hipped youth
when hopeful bondsmaid to the new.
"You'll never know," she said, "how much
we talked of you and hoped those days
when you dreamed here of Helen, whales,
telegraph harps and scarlet A's;
dreams more passionately pure
than one of us could ever have,
we knew with deep humility.
For elder is always wickeder
than young and worships innocence."

"As ignorance should worship elder
knowledge."

       "What we two could have done."
And then again the silence fell,
in the room and out the windows
where the homely rural landscape
stretched that used to hold around
me while I slept, no house-wife yet.
"It all changed then," she said and nodded
at the unhealed wounds where I
once slit my wrists and nearly died.
"Your hands have been so clumsy since.
Why did you try to kill yourself?"
It hurt to let her speak of it,
but lying galliard on the pallet bed,
so strong and fair though starved and sad,
with blossoms in her bloody hair,
she slant me held with Renoir

eyes and, "Why?" insisted, "bleed
the little bit you'd brought from home?
You wanted to stay virgin-dumb?
You were afraid you might grow up?
Miss, Miss?" she smiling spat.
I bowed my head. I didn't know.
Only the wounds had never healed
and I'd since grown, not wrong—O, surely
just differently to what had been
presumed. And yet too fat to enter
in the chamber of my youth.
But she could stroll about at home
there in her make-shift clacking shoes
and recognize her image in
the rivery old glass. O, more,
always more beautiful the elder
is than young.

            "Why did you come?
Why come and torment me?"

"I simply came to see, for I
am very tired now and ill
and thought to leave my treasures here
before I die. Do you think that you
could ever find a place for them?"

I did not say. I heard the orphans
back from school and went to fix
their lunch and have not seen her since.
But from my Bendix and my Monel
metal sink such strange thoughts jump
at me and dance as make me dizzy:
as that it's I who's dead, dead
though so active at my chores.
And soon she will appear, dressed

in a dress of mine, re-made, and young
with energy of mind and bone
as I have never known. She'll scold
the children like a foreign aunt
and make them put away their toys,
learn their lessons, dust her treasures.
While I still flit about the stove,
a short-breathed, plump, suburban ghost.
I almost hope that that is so:
for even the fat despair and if
it's she who's died and lies
there in my little room—the one thing
that she never had at home—
by old sanguinity I'll not
outlast her long but flop down on
my clean linoleum and no one
at all then to scold or spoil
my poor, twice-orphanned girls and boys.

SURREAL

Inside, the ship's great ribs arched close and leaped
    To an obscurity of smoke.
    Its lateral planked walls were broke
By lancet windows bended to the peak.

And narrow-niched before each lance, a fair
    Long-leggèd little daughter sat
    Upon her long-robed mother's lap
And gravely flickered cards in solitaire.

Unmindful of the little girls that played
    So mild, down down from far above
    The women gazed and did not move,
But all the vasty hull to quiet laid.

Gay, and his dust-pan's clatter like a fall
    Of bells, a gray-curled delicate
    Young sacristan made mention that
Of Holy Meditation it was called.

TO CLEAN UP

Let me be house-wife to my mind,
    That room I entered as a child
And, lodger till I die, must find
    My home to renovate though not re-build.

First to tear down the clumsy walls
    I reared when young to comfort me
Against its size, that narrow stall
    Each thought and cross-bar continuity.

Throw out the quaintly painted chests
    My parents lent when I was poor
In things and feared its airy emptiness.
    But search them first and quick restore

To use what diapered towel,
    Silver bowl or plate of frugal
Pewter, hand-worn handled trowel
    May be a right and loved memorial.

All foreign tricks and gauds, knick-knack
    Treasures of tourist youth, throw out;
All unproved borrowings that hark me back
    To years of schools and visiting about.

Clearance bares the rats' long envies,
    The spider female's deathly lust,
Dung-footed laziness of sleepy flies,
    Regret in velvet piles of dust.

Still faith will scatter filth and lime
    The walls till cleanly vaulted, low
And white they spring to light and shine
    With warmth from ample sunny windows.

Not large nor rare nor beautiful
    My home, but fit at least at last
For what I own of rich and useful
    Textures. Some I have made, the best

Pre-empted from the common store
    By right of love. A curved recess
Will hold the bench where I, a poor
    Magician, imperilled would-be princess

Transmute or spin my straw to gold.
    That straw my bed, let night stars stream
Upon my sleep and breed, not old
    Nightmares, but passionate prophetic dreams.

One thing's to add—a marble court
    Like Ovid's, under a scarlet awning,
Where sometimes friends and loves consort
    With juleps or carafes of wine.

Thus quit-clause temper, not de-base,
    The many-mansioned tenement requires—
That even garret roomers celebrate,
    Rehearse and learn by fact their loneliness.

TOWARDS—FROM NEW ENGLAND

From grass-lined pool, his face looks up.
    One does for both
Of us, but he in the live-oak
    Attends a flute.

Cousin to Tobit's journey-friend,
    His presence lends
My thoughts the soft and precious awe
    That lovers use.

He formless broods in violet
    Over the pale
And crackling pennants of the corn
    Before a rain.

And he exists in difference
    Between the same—
As honeysuckle wild or sober,
    There or here.

When fall's banal forebodings set
    My teeth on edge,
Like rosy-gold persimmon lies
    He dangles high

And leaves me plucking after him;
    Serener days,
He's fall's own flesh-sweet smell that flows
    Along the ground.

And he's when metaphor strikes home,
    Or when a poem
Bowls down all nine pre-conceptions
    For acceptance.

But still, no *he*—no, nor abstract
    God-head, neither.—
Perhaps he is my self in time,
    For he is most

The some times when I wholly am;
    When sights oblique
To others' figures find despair
    Irrelevant.

O, seldom, suave, whose merest fig-
    frond hand on blue
's a good these apple eaters fear-
    fully refuse;

Magnolia grandiflora, you
    Are no cozy
Sickness that a train could cure
    But farther, huge.

OR THIS, PERRAULT—

So here it is, he said, and left
his bride and beauty free of the castle's
beds of flowers, free of its middens;
free to chance and choice with only
night and day and sun and moon
to clock and curtail her devices.

Whether for days or years he'd gone,
the time seemed short before a dusk wind
to her terrace brought, up caught
from the far woods, the far off horn
of his return.
                        Ah, then she turns
and runs, runs from the flower beds
and middens, climbs the stairs above
the battlements, the crooking, climbing
stairs to the half-forgotten room.
And, half-forgotten there, she finds
her murdered selves like dresses folded
on the shelves, a-glimmer one
by one in the dusky wall-less room
where only starlight comes.
                        Childhood
brothers rage and weep and Anne
laments. Come down, they call, O sister
dear. He's killed enough, they yell.

But bride has deafly shut the door
and private cries, Here first he'll come
with blazing eyes and azure beard
and groin. Careless of rags or best,
she lays her last dress on the last
bare shelf and at the knife-
edge of the room awaits the horn.

FROM

OUT IN THE OPEN

TO APOLLO MUSAGETES

Farewell, farewell
Who was the best of me.
My mind's turned Quakerish
And silent sits
Possessed by grey vacuity.
Bunched like silly swallows on a line,
Presaging rain,
Words preen, shove, twist and twit
But will not ever burst up into the wild air again,
Nor jet-dive down that narrow, nested chimney-flue of mine.
Jet-power and precision-sight are gone,
Long gone.
Farewell.
Say I strung gauds to an almost poem;
Rhymes, rhythms, images contrived;
In fact, a còmpleat mechanism nifti-
ly devised
And that pleased the critics;
Remembering thee, I could no less
Than hate that seeming
And mourn again the warm, the fleshed
And quiet breathing
That, with thy help, I'd sometimes come by.
Farewell.
Say I confessed my every grievous lack
Of body, spirit, mind and corrected all—
Shored with six virtues each sagged fault—
No effort brought, nor none will get thee back.
Thou cam'st in deed the sun
To pour me down and gild with courage, brightness, gay
persuasions.

And goest too
Like him, ghost-
ing me to farthermost Antipodes,
Native
To live
There with some pale, timid, forlorn race
Of twilit savages
That's never seen thy face.
Farewell.
Who, having seen, can't keep thee
Lose heart even to weep thee.
Farewell, farewell.

GUILT

Patient and small as life, our minor betrayals
Await us in the ante-room to Hell;
Mild creditors of fear and snobbery,
    And lazy cruelty.

At ten, how eloquent we were to teach
That boy shame for country shoes and speech.
His blue eyes, brilliant with astonished tears,
    Illuminate the years.

An old black nurse took ferry, trolley, bus
To call on his beautiful child, now all grown-up;
Grown-up too vain to doff her busyness
    Before his tiredness.

And what of those lonely women who found in Death,
Not us, the punctual friend? To right and left,
The benches fill with our gentle victims; not
    Insistent, not forgot.

Called from sole and scrod,
Chef picks up the phone;
Catches words like God's
From it and hurls it down.
My wife?!
Sprung from wrung bowels, the cry
Is quick disguised
By young and loyal waiters who
Toss pots and clatter pans;
Then, still in the blood-spattered apron
Of his trade, support him to a landing
Off the stairs
And seat him.
Grieve here, they say, but don't disturb
The diners who have reached liqueurs,
That profitable course.
Grieve, grieve at your ease, old man,
But do not howl.
He squats on the chair
And does not howl,
Just stares.
The while, on bloody apron gray as wash,
On face and hair of soggy ash,
On an old beat-up clothes-horse,
The young waiters wait—
Brown-skinned, black-chevelured, sinewed, muscled—
Two to a side.
And now another mounts the stair.
Cup-bearer, brandy in his hand,
His knee is bent
To climb, to make a present.
And the light shifts.

You'd say someone had varnished it.
You'd say an antiquarian Masaccio,
Stumbling upon an ancient garden statue,
    Some remnant of the Greeks
    Weathered to low relief,
(Silenus or a garden variety of Grief)
Had set it on its pedestal and set
His bronze-eyed cinque-cento boys round it.
Bronze-muscled and bronze-eyed,
    Adept with knife and rod,
These young Guineas recognize a god,
        Still.
    Courage, old stone, they murmur,
    (who once cold-chisel sleeked like us
    To features will be reived from us,
        Too)
        Don't howl,
    (Who are our own).
But let us go now to fetch liqueurs.
    Back at their jobs,
    Suave gestures,
    Sorrow-spattered eyes
Abstracted to a past they can't recall,
    Speak of a statue fallen
    In a neglected garden,
    Of abandoned sepultures.

WHEN SNOW FALLS

It's as though
I had been very happy
Once, maybe was often happy,
        And there was snow;

For years ago,
From warmth and strength of nurse or lover lean-
ing me window-ward, I'd always seen
        The falling snow.

Now sole specific
For my ill, this flock-meal white has roused
That old expectancy; unhoused
        Serene Atlantic

Bays of being,
Lately forgot; happiness, of late
Forgot. Chaos of face and thing erased,
        Abstracts of seeing

Hold me still.
This mildest magister very air
Of the years' strata has deftly unlayered
        And tranquil

My spirit walks
In pathèd sky fields. Royal meander.
Pleasaunce of saints and nature-worshippers;
        So bred, so taught

  To high estate
They're gravelled, like rich heirs, by its lack.
But I'm unused to, poor in fact
  In God or lakes.

  A human gesture
Lacking, on grey unhurried clouds I wait
Must patiently, on snow-fall for this late
  Late investiture.

A KIND OF PROGRESS

There came a time when bird
Talk enticed her wholly from words.
She who had loved a page full
Of print found all that dull
Now beside the distraction of eaves-dropping
On their gossiping;

A phrase here and there
Caught contented her.

After the mild crisis
A breeze stirs in the iris,
She found that a stricter waving—
Invisible, inaudible saving
To one who in do-nothing quiet waited—told
Of earth-shaker mole

Pursuant of interests
At the feet of the lilies.

Frost comes out of the ground
With an over-all tinkling sound
As thousands of little crystals
Crack, and shattered fall;
As thousands of little winters go in a long
Delicate explosion.

And she would linger at the garden
Brink a long time and listen.

These were wonders all, but not quite miracles;
Wonders often given
To plowmen or countrywomen.
Not for the busy, earth keeps for the lonely
And idle only

(Already feckless as saints)
An especial grace.

So—
An April when the sun
Shone hotter than in June,
And the air too still to stir
One dead leaf from off another,
She heard, like twiggy fires' snap and flow,
The grass grow.

To no plowman, to her brother
Of earth's pensioners,

To the huntsman ran: I heard
It. It wasn't birds,
Nor moles, nor frost going.
It was the grass growing.
Silence, except—and warm and quiet . . . Calm-faced
Who had been in that place,

He said, smiling as if back
There, I'm so glad you heard that.

THE UNPOWERFUL

Wood scored by wind and rain
Where yellow sleeps cross-grain—
Cat and the grey bench mould
The circumambient air.
If they could lead me to pretend a fair
Terrain of meadow fold-
ing round a square stone house,
Urned terraces, wide steps, the sea—
Transient as magic though—
'Twould comfort me.

Each thing radiates
A force proportionate
Against the invading air.
By mere in-tension
And of their opulence, a sea and mansion
Could easy bend and flare
The meagre forms for making
A weathered bench, an indolent animal.
So moderate a feigning
Is usual.

Small things have ado
To stay as they are. Into
No larger can mine reach
Me than a narrow garden,
A narrow house incontinently wooden.
Ought I estates beseech
Of their poverty?
Though hemmed in, weighed on, ought I
Ask cat for the sea?

WHERE IS IT THAT WE GO?

A sea is always there,
So pale, so soft.
As brushy rim of air,
Or film of silken cloth
In lightest foldings fall'n, it makes the island.

From porcelain sky there dangles
A Crown embossed,
Argent massif fork handle.
A pendulum that's stopped
Half up it hangs, a handsome ornament.

And round us, sparsely scattered,
Qualities—
Say Faith or Courage—mattered
Rear in granite masses;
And at the same time airy abstracts are.

So we, two statued figures
On the plain,
With robed and noble gestures
Personate, contain
A grave and loving, silent conversation.

Though small silk square of Fear
Drift by our calm,
And though we see and hear
It; palm in hooded palm,
We still embody bright serenities.

Nor not just you you are,
But several;
My uncle, as Chinese scholar
By a waterfall,
Extends his own perspective from your temple . . .

We rifle two-thirds of our lives
To people this land
And clothe it; so to arrive
Mayhap at its essence, trans-
Substance layman and reversed albeit.

Cry the Psyche doctors,
Eroticism;
Decry they should not viator
So far come, so be-prismed
And brilliant—Eros or other—with instances

Of that desirable country,
Also ours,
Whose radiant geography,
On lucky days, outpours,
Cascades its sweetness on our waking hours.

ANNE'S WOODS

Boughed by swart hemlock and rocketing
Beech, open as if kindly pathed,
Yet tricky somewhere as in fairy tales—

> I think I don't grieve for you now,
> My tropic sister. But still
> There're no other woods so especial to me.

In April, sweet white violets
Would force their ways through tissued leaves;
Fern fiddleheads uncurled and fountained
Hellebore poured primal green.

> See, Kate—interrupting our gossip.

And we agreed that not fragilities
Of flowers but this, this shaped and stalwart
Green, and of the deep-piled candled
Moss, tempered the old woods' mournfulness.
And I'd not mention gaieties
Of young and hasty leaves athwart
A time-blacked bole for fear
You'd break the spray and take it home.

> But my god, Anne—today you could
> Rip up the whole forest and make off
> With it, for all I'd care.

The woods were lightened, too, where shafts of sun-shine
Plumbed the brown-foiled waterfall,
Dissolved the sparkles of its froth,
Or turned a dirty fungus white as bone.

In summer we will find (your voice strangered
Words; a grocery list would seem
Half-heard, half-dreamed—an old mysterious
Spell now powerless) warty Morels,
Agaricus Campestris in the glades,
Inky Coprinus's drooped umbrellas,
Green Russula and gold Boletus,
The Lepiotas, smooth or parasoled,
And delicate Chanterelle—all good to eat.
And I will show you both the Amanitas;
White, the forest angel, called Of Death,
And Orange, Caesar's, the Imperial.
I'll show you . . .
                          Powerless, indeed.

And there was moody brightness where
The prismed sun pricked at the laminates
Of mica lodged in granite scarps.
But light so pierced, flickered, fretted's scarcely
Radiant. All ways dark these woods were
And mournful as fixed in some enchantment
Unresolved to good or evil, cruel
Or kind, and very very quiet.
The waterfall fell muffled on the moss.
Sometimes a company of sparrows whirled
(As in the fall brown leaves are blown)
With a soft whir to the trees' tops;
Then dropped back one by one, small birds,
To the leafy floor. Sometimes, far off,
Far like an old car revved too hard,
The great grouse drummed . . .

What was it, Kate, you asked me once
(Your tawny-foiled eyes a-flicker)
What in our childhood, in our growing-up
That made me love you more than any
Man or child I've ever had?

PRODIGAL LOVE

The little beech tree, pricked and pried
Out of its native wood,
So late, so roughly moved,
So like to die,
Enlists our tenderest and rescue mood.

We feed and water it. Each day
Inspect its reddening twigs
For one bud swelled too big
For shard to stay:
O, little beech tree, will you die or live?

When this—so pale, so fair, so frail—
Chooses to live, then we
Like chosen priests believe
'Twas our travail
That fluted out its brilliant peel of leaves.

MIDDAY AND ALL SAINTS' CHURCH

(*Peterborough, N.H.*)

These enjoin ear-split attention, choose
You or not. Our stately little church cuts loose
      Then with a vertical
      Into sidereal
Racket that beats out all the horizontal
      Efforts of ambulances, squad
      Cars, fire trucks and hot-rods

Combined. Bing-*bong* -bong, bong-bong, bong. The sounds
Can hardly be said to 'float' up or 'waft'. They pound
      Up. And demure architectural
      Gem shows for an arsenal
Whence the bronze and silver cannon balls
      Of Our Lord's artillery
      Make merry.

Not to plead or accuse, not for a special birth
Or death, just that the glory of His earth
      Be announced,
      Clearly pronounced
A few minutes every day, these balls bounce—
      Detonated bronze and silver—
      Up and after one another.

A salvo of grace! So winning, local tradesmen
Even might look alert at lunch and listen.
      But, You get used
      To it, they excuse
Themselves and dummy up. They simply refuse
      To be taken in
      By this anarchism.

Our pastor, who's lived a life-time under fire,
Scrapes his chair, though, hunches a little higher,
       And digs his old Greek text
       Like a table of ballistics.
From 'probable error', from 'brackets' and 'stress',
       The every day uproar still beguiles
       Him and he smiles.

BACCHANAL

The bitch, the bitched, the bugger, the bewildered,
        The murderer and the murdered
            Form our circle.
Betrayer and betrayed are one.
        When each the same has done,
            Distinction's gone.
So I knife him while you knife me,
        Embraced in the Conga reel
            Of treachery.
Truth and Love, keep far away.
        This is not your day,
            Nor not fit play
For you. Keep to the high rock ledges.
        Down here, a catty knowledge
            Of softness spreads
Across the dance, then calls the round.
        Its fur pads glance, then pound
            The dizzy ground.
What joy to join in that great dancing,
        What rebirth in forgetting
            Everything
But that, as we drown from individual
        Sense to general,
            Desire is all.
Bright Truth, sweet Love, you never helped
        So well the terrible surfeit
            Of our self.

THE TRUTHFUL PAST

At last, the King gets tired and abdicates.
His Queen, puzzled to withstand the wanton
    Games Pretenders invite her to,
Invokes the faith old letters predicate.
  Alack! Those time-sealed royal words, still young,
    Still chisel-edged to rive her through,
Betrayal sing. As if, no human prince
Now old, but some superber stranger roving—
    Some frolic god in huntsman's cap—
Had stumbled upon her, there by the flowering quince,
And knelt him down; then shoved the virgin-loving
    Unicorn from off her lap.

THE PARTRIDGE TREE

In dusk of rain,
Two lovers watched two partridge birds
In a hawthorn tree.
Slim boughs were scarletted with berries,
Perched evenly
The delicate-necked dim partridges.
Stroking her hair,
"The gun's in the rack," he smilingly murmured,
But neither stirred.

In dusk of dawn,
The hawthorn reached the second floor
And birds were four
That walked therein, ravaging
The scarlet berries.
"We might make pets of them," he said.
"Partridges,"
Said she, "though silent birds and good,
Prefer wild food."
And laughing asked, "Do not we, too?"

But one more topless flight, they thought,
Would show the tree
Espaliered huge across noon's bluest
Clarity,
Its slim boughs Christmassèd, and crammed
With partridges.
But compassion for each other gentled
Them and taught
There'd not come more growth to house or tree
Nor more birds be.

A WAY OF BEING

My life, this man once said,
Is like a book. The wife I had
And the other one, a girl
In summered Maryland, my captain
At the war, the war, the crows
My boyhood spent shooting, Paris
In miserable August. I sometimes look
Them over but can never
Wish them back, continuing, or different;
For they are stories.

So we, then, are but fictions.
What we have been or done's but his
Imagining. Paris
Is brown.
We're all this man's creations
And it is to his glory that we tend,
For he's the hero.
Yet we will get our due;
For he's not bulged himself as Valor, Love,
Nor shrunk a life's magnificence to them,
But peopled, polyhedral keeps
His story.

Patient of the end—saving
It like dessert of childhood, savorous
Promises implicit in the past,
Let us dally with this banquet that it last.
Let us wait here;
While he still holds the page erect between
Our storied yesterday—tomorrow not yet read—
Wait here and learn a little

How we were; learn how
Though cruel as Iago, false
As Cressida,
His noble rendering ennobles us.

Stay for a long moment with the page
Thus poised, maître.
And let us pluck at virtue
By your means.
Artists are few and works of art
And this will soon enough be done—
Done, done, loosed and scattered—
Gone.
While we, illiterately transcribed page
Or half-remembered phrase
Will blow down dirty streets
As from a golden age.

NIGHT-PIECE

(*after reading the* Chanson de Roland)

Lie still, be quiet.
Put your head down, shut your eyes.
I'm tired, too,
And can't much longer swear to see you through.
So, so—bestow yourself to quietude.

The shadowed, sinister and deep defile,
Strewn with grey rocks, strewn
With the years' potsherds and today's,
(Go, go—go fast)
The pass
Will open on a wide plume-clouded plain
A-loud with horns,
On azure, vert and argentine.
And you,
Ragged your guidon, though, and hacked your sword
May King it there with feudal
Dreams; easy at last and royal.
If Aude the Fair and Peers of France you summon
Or Gibbon-buttocked demons
Will, beau sire, be up to you.
Right now—get through.
Go, enter at the door to France.
Go sleep, beau roi—I keep the pass.

My eyelids need be propped.
I can but little longer stay
Awake to see you through.
And once you're gone; no knight and Sister's Son
But recenter; as surly sad, anarchic
Dynamiter, I'll plant my stick and run.

Run through the same, yet different for each one,
Defile of rocks so grey and cedars tenebrous
To my own door to France.

Although, by like minds photographed,
In curious montage our dreams may meet
And merge; you and I'll not meet.
For wise men say
That whom we dream of
We have ceased to love,
People the dream kingdoms how we may.
And should we, like Aude and the peers, answer a summon-
    ing
To endure a sort of pretty murdering?
Beau sire, my friend, let us go through together,
King and dynamiter,
And then separate.
And leave our loves stay here,
Estopped in the outrageous pass;
Leave them to gossip, play cards, drink the night out;
So they ensure our returning
Paths lead to each other's morning.

A JOURNEY

1

Thereat, he smiles. And big with the lordly strength
Of passiveness, he stretches him full length;
   A Country
   For her discovery.

While she, his blue-eyed—faithful immigrant
Or facile tourist—dallies hesitant
   Before happiness
   So much like holiness.

Mists of dawn en-island tops of trees.
Black pines striate the pallid hills that seas
   Or serpents seem, or lariats—
   Now undulant, now flat.

A moment more she gazes wide and stands
Most delicate in awe before this Land.
   Then starts on her journey,
   Her destiny.

2

The sun is up and she has reached the wood.
From hand to hand, as if not they but she stood
    Still, the trees bring
    Her first fruits of spring.

But past years' leaves, tissue and stiff brown parchment,
Churn and confound her steps like an element.
    Nor can the carved arbutus
    Or beech buds' spiralled flutes

Cancel the sorrow of their waves' sussurance.
Small birds' uneasy chirps give reassurance
    Solely to one another
    As Brother, they whisper, Brother.

Sure, sovran disappointment waits for all
Who mapless, uninsured, not even called
    For certain, essay
    Love's difficult way.

Still she knows the true explorer looks
For what is there. And not most epic books
    Can gloss
    Either his loss

Or his magnificent reward. (The seven
Cities not pyrites turned, but golden
    Stayed
    For those whom Death waylaid).

3
Up into noon of day and summer crawls,
Where sun in goldenest abandon's sprawled;
    Where nothing stops her vision
    But horizon.

Not now imagined seas or snakes or ropes;
It's very mountains tumble, slope on slope,
    Cloud-blear,
    Ice-clear,

Imperious statements of mortality.
(If words though, louder, foreigner, more free
    Than human ear
    Can hear).

Sick, scared, infatuate, she may guess
Into this coldly guarded privateness
    Of a man's estate,
    But never penetrate.

Passionate hurricanes of Ana-Purna,
Thin-aired, abstract prayers that flow from Lama
    Territory
    Minatory

Are as much to her, far-eyed far-voyager,
As to any doll-housed valley-villager;
    To all
    Whose powers are medial.

4

Strained, drained, eyes shut to retain, to remember
If never to know, she turns. Turns to September,
>To the peace
>Of growth's surcease,

And the afternoon half gone. Easy the paths
Now, broad and very still. Blueness wafts
>Between the trees,
>Between the dangling leaves,

Between meadow and swale. Quietened
By fall's thus mild, thus endless-seeming end,
>She walks light-errant,
>Zig-zag with currents

Of fall's sweet smell like flesh in sex that streams
As out of sobbing gulfs of love or dreams,
>Or rush up
>Through crevices in the heavy dusk.

5

But lulla-blue dissolves with sun's declension.
And quick and quivering she flairs fox-season.
  Skies are delicate,
  Grasses fritillate,

Trees spread sombre beams a-loft the snow.
In single file the little fox tracks go,
  Nicked
  By tail-tip.

Candid and huntsman here, the tracks entice
Her toward the grove where pale fox-fires light
  A questionable, wintry
  Revelry.

Hand in paw we'll prance, sings Fox, the feral
Pleasures due half-starved, half-devil animals.
  But she—bough-barred, moon-rapt,
  A-point though—stands fast.

6

First circle's turned and now the churn begins
To splash up winter, summer, fall; morning,
      The noons of day and night,
      Both twilights.

Wittol spring alone, the green on blue
Of beech buds' spiralled flutes, is gone for good.
      And she forgets
      What it is she regrets.

Kaleidoscope of years and climates marks
A day, not place or season, bright or dark.
      (Each day's confected by each man
      As best he can).

Yet Judas-springs of childhood crowd from deep
In the Land's resources. Rousing from fretted sleep
      To call her Lover;
      Mother,

She calls . . . And still no past, no holiday
In far countree, no child can long delay
      Her from
      The journey that is home.

She stays no where, but ever new frontiers
Makes or finds. Inveterate pioneer
      She owns from day to day
      Naught but the long trajet.

But manna, largesse, presents, fair reward
If he, her Land, her Love turn and come toward
      Her and, O rare, they walk
      Together for a while and talk.

7

When, old lioness, she clambers—grey,
Rheumatic, blue-and inward-eyed with age—
      To that first eminence
      Of youthful fear, and thence

Her different sight discerns those Himalayas
Lapped and encroached by flowery green savannahs;
      The change but adds a variable,
      An illimitable

Further statement of the real adventure
That shrivels her journey to a detour;
      Makes what she's seen seem small,
      What learned provincial

Lore that Fox or Deer-Mouse profit by
To live, and well perhaps, yet not travel by.
      She knows no seasons now.
      Though he, her Love, now crouch

Beside her, eyes avoid. They lie near,
Alone and cold as two carved stones, and rear
      Blind heads to snuff a sweet-
      ness left behind their reach.